Girls Science Club

Cool Engineering Activities for Girls

by Heather E. Schwartz

Consultant:
Lana Fountain Flakes
Director of Membership Initiatives
Society of Women Engineers

CAPSTONE PRESS
a capstone imprint

Snap Books are published by Capstone Press,
1710 Roe Crest Drive, North Mankato, Minnesota 56003.
www.capstonepub.com

Copyright © 2012 by Capstone Press, a Capstone imprint.
All rights reserved.
No part of this publication may be reproduced in whole or in part, or stored in a retrieval system,
or transmitted in any form or by any means, electronic, mechanical, photocopying, recording,
or otherwise, without written permission of the publisher.
For information regarding permission, write to Capstone Press,
1710 Roe Crest Drive, North Mankato, Minnesota 56003.

 Books published by Capstone Press are manufactured with paper containing at least 10 percent post-consumer waste.

Library of Congress Cataloging-in-Publication Data
Schwartz, Heather E.
Cool engineering activities for girls / by Heather E. Schwartz.
  p. cm.—(Snap books. Girls science club)
Includes bibliographical references and index.
Summary: "Provides step-by-step instructions for activities demonstrating engineering concepts and scientific explanations for the concepts presented"—Provided by publisher.
 ISBN 978-1-4296-7677-9 (library binding)
 ISBN 978-1-4296-8021-9 (paperback)
 1. Engineering—Experiments—Juvenile literature. 2. Girls—Education—Juvenile literature. 3. Science projects—Juvenile literature. I. Title. II. Series.
 TA149.S436 2012
 607—dc23   2011031376

Editorial Credits
Editor: Jennifer Besel
Designer: Heidi Thompson
Photo Stylist: Sarah Schuette
Scheduler: Marcy Morin
Production Specialist: Kathy McColley

Photo Credits: All images Capstone Studio: Karon Dubke, except: iStockphoto: Anthia Cumming, cover (top), Doug Cannell, cover (bolt); Shutterstock: blue67design (hand drawn design), Goodluz, 5, urfin, cover (bottom left)

Printed in the United States of America in North Mankato, Minnesota.
052017   010554R

Table of Contents

Engineering Your World   4

Litter Grabber   6

Fresher Fruit   8

Paper Table   10

Carnival Secret Revealed!   12

World-Saving Water Filter   14

Finding a Quiet Spot   16

New Jewelry from Old CDs   18

Tie-Dyed Engineering   20

S'mores from the Sun   22

Alarming Fun   26

Glossary   30

Read More   31

Internet Sites   31

Index   32

Engineering Your World

Have you ever wanted something that hasn't been invented yet? A machine that loads the dishwasher? Or a cookie so packed with nutrients it counts as a vegetable? Some might call these dreams wishful thinking. But daydreaming is the first step in engineering. Throughout history engineers have come up with some amazing **innovations**. They're behind inventions such as the bionic arm, roller coasters, and even wireless phones.

When engineers encounter problems, they dream up solutions. Want to see how engineering can change your world? The projects in this book will have you engineering recyclable furniture, funky clothes, and more. But here's the catch. If you think of a better way to make something, go for it! Thinking creatively means you're thinking like a real engineer.

innovation: a new invention

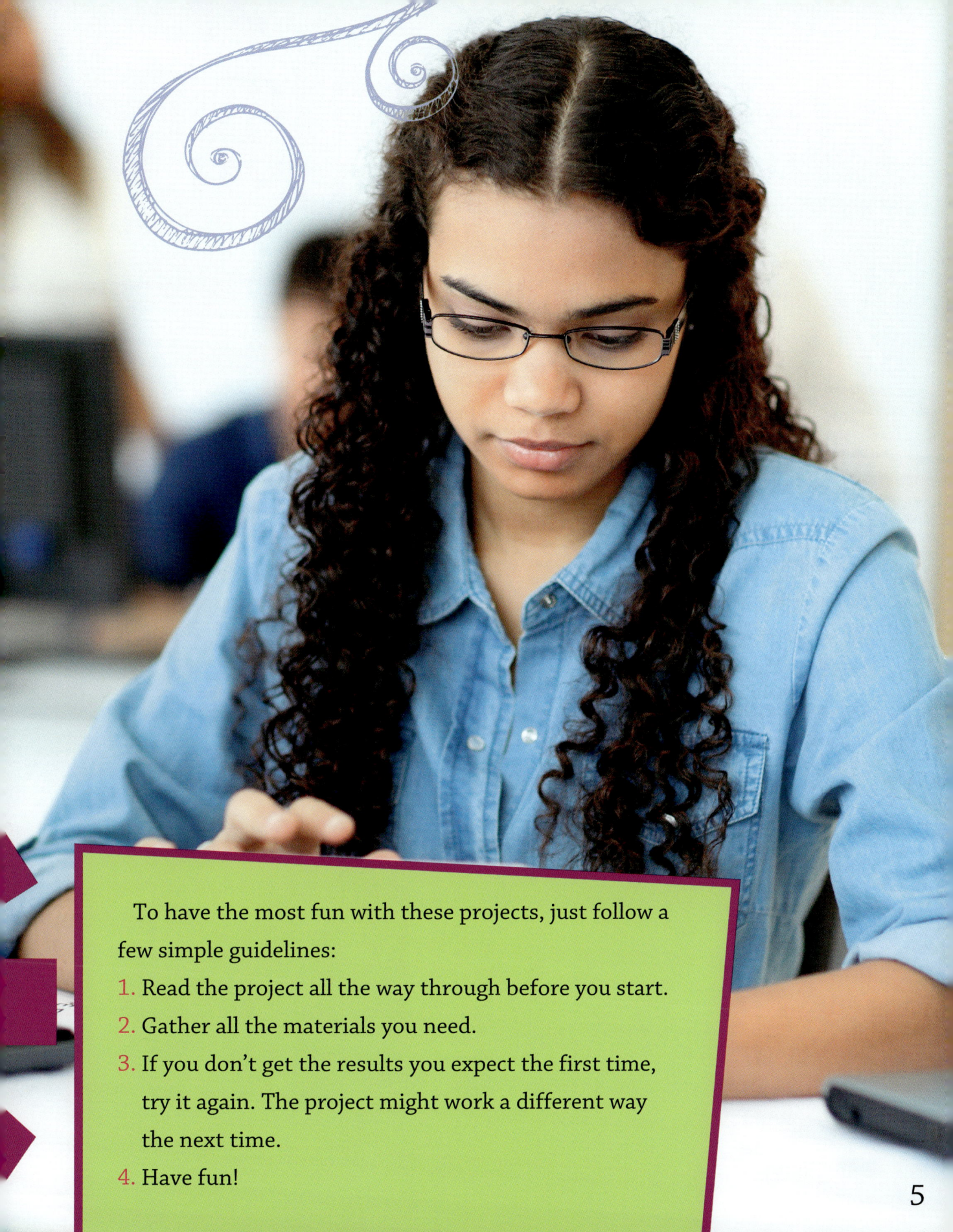

To have the most fun with these projects, just follow a few simple guidelines:
1. Read the project all the way through before you start.
2. Gather all the materials you need.
3. If you don't get the results you expect the first time, try it again. The project might work a different way the next time.
4. Have fun!

Litter Grabber

Walking by your local park, you spot some trash under the slide. Hiking through the woods, you see an old soda can by a tree. Get your science groove on, and make a tool to help clean up your favorite places.

Supplies

- pliers
- wire hanger
- wire cutters
- ruler
- duct tape
- wooden dowel, ¼ inch (.6 centimeter) diameter; 3½ feet (1 meter) long
- plastic PVC pipe, 1 inch (2.5 cm) diameter; 3 feet (.9 m) long
- a rolled ball of newspaper about the size of a tennis ball

1. Use pliers to straighten the hanger's hook.

2. Have an adult use wire cutters to cut the hanger's bottom about 2 inches (5 cm) from each corner.

3. Push in on the corners to squeeze the two cut ends of the wire together. They do not need to touch but should form a V shape.

4. Wrap the two cut ends with duct tape to pad the ends.

5. Duct tape the top of the hanger to one end of the dowel. Cover the end of the wire completely with tape.

6. Slide the free end of the dowel inside the PVC pipe so it sticks out like a handle.

7. Point the padded ends toward the ground. Test your grabber by picking up a ball of newspaper. Pull the dowel to make the ends grab the paper ball. Push the dowel to open the grabber and release the trash.

Insider Info

Each material used to make the grabber has a specific function. The dowel inside the pipe holds the hanger. When the dowel is pushed, the grabber ends slide out of the pipe and open up. When the dowel is pulled, the wires are dragged inside the pipe and squeezed together. This squeezing motion grabs onto the trash.

The duct tape helps keep the trash in the grabber. Duct tape adds texture to the grabber ends. This rough surface creates **friction**. When the grabber ends rub against the trash, friction helps keep the trash from falling out. Where the grabber touches the trash is the contact area. Duct tape adds contact area to the ends. The more contact area there is, the more friction there will be. The trash won't slip out until you're ready to drop it in the garbage can.

friction: a force created when two objects rub together; friction slows down objects

Fresher Fruit

Bananas are fabulous snacks. But they get brown, mushy, and messy fast. Is there a way to package those bananas so they won't go bad so quickly?

Supplies

- 5 green bananas
- 2 brown lunch bags
- scissors
- 2 cardboard shoe boxes with lids
- notebook
- pen

1. Put one banana in a brown paper bag. Roll the top to close the bag.

2. Use scissors to cut three holes in two sides of the other paper bag. Put a banana inside, leaving the top open.

3. Put a banana in a cardboard box and cover it.

4. Poke three holes in each side of the other box and lid. Put a banana inside and cover it.

5. Place all of the packaged bananas in the same cool, dry area away from sunlight. Put the last banana in the same area as the others but leave it out of all packaging.

6. For the next two weeks, check the bananas at the same time every day. In your notebook, keep a chart to track changes in color, smell, and mushiness. By the end of your experiment, you'll know which packaging keeps bananas freshest the longest.

Insider Info

Did you know that bananas breathe? It's true! Bananas take in oxygen and release carbon dioxide. This process, called respiration, causes bananas to ripen. When bananas ripen, they produce a gas called ethylene. This gas **accelerates** the ripening process. In the packaging with holes, the bananas ripened fastest. They got mushy fast because the packaging let oxygen in and also trapped the ethylene near the banana.

The dry, airtight packaging kept oxygen out. Without the oxygen flowing in, ripening was delayed. However the ethylene was still trapped near the banana. No packaging at all kept the banana yellow longest. Even though it was exposed to oxygen, the fruit ripened slower because ethylene wasn't trapped nearby.

accelerate: to speed up

Paper Table

Need a table for your movie night snacks? With a little engineering know-how, you can make a table yourself—no hammer or saw required.

Supplies

- 20 full sheets of newspaper
- masking tape
- paint, glitter, and other decorative materials
- 12 inch (30 cm) square piece of thick cardboard

1. Layer four sheets of newspaper on top of each other. Roll diagonally from corner to corner into a tube. Secure with tape. Repeat this step four more times to create a total of five tubes.

2. Bend two of the tubes into triangles of equal size. Secure with tape.

3. Tape one end of each straight tube to the points on one triangle.

4. Tape the other ends of the tubes to the points on the second triangle. This shape will be the table's base.

5. Paint and decorate the cardboard square and paper tube base. Let them dry completely.

6. Place the base upright so one triangle is on the floor, and one is in the air. Place the cardboard on the top triangle. Secure with tape underneath.

Insider Info

What would happen if you had built the table with just one leg? It would probably fall right over. But imagine that you got it to stand, and you set something heavy on it. The weight would crush the leg, and the table would collapse. The triangle-shaped tubes in this project **stabilize** the table so it won't fall over. But they also help with load distribution. The legs spread out the force of weight. When an object is placed on the three-legged table, the object's weight doesn't press on only one leg. Instead, the weight's force is spread among all three legs. All the legs work together to support the object.

If you want to make an even stronger table, try changing the base's shape. For example, make a square-shaped base to hold the table together. Then attach four legs. The weight of an object would be distributed among more legs. So your table could hold even more movie night treats.

stabilize: to make firm and steady

Carnival Secret Revealed!

Some carnival games look so easy. Then you pay to play and find they can't be beat. Study the science behind this balloon trick to win despite the odds.

Supplies

- 4 red balloons
- 4 blue balloons
- cardboard display board
- clear tape
- tape measure
- masking tape
- 6 sharp-tip darts

1 Blow up two red balloons about three-quarters full of air. They should appear full, but still feel squishy. Blow up two blue balloons full of air. They should look smooth and shiny.

2 Prop the display board on a table against a wall. Make sure it is not near any windows or other breakable items.

3 Tape the balloons in a line at eye level on the display board.

4 Measure 8 feet (2.4 m) from the board. Mark your spot with masking tape.

5 Stand at your mark. With adult supervision, throw the darts straight at the balloons. Did the balloons pop when you hit them? Were any hard or impossible to pop?

6 Now blow up two more red balloons three quarters full of air. Blow up two more blue balloons full of air.

7 Remove the other balloons, and tape the new ones to the board.

8 Stand back at your mark. Now throw the darts so they hit the balloons on the top, not straight on. You'll need to throw the darts at an upward angle so they arc down toward the balloons. Are they easier to pop now?

Insider Info

When the darts hit the full blue balloons, the balloons most likely popped. The latex of a full balloon is stretched and stressed. The force of the dart burst the balloon's thin and weak material.

When your darts hit the partially full red balloons, you may have had more trouble. As carnival workers know, balloons are harder to pop when their latex isn't stressed. Rather than piercing it, the dart tip bounces off.

But you can beat the game even with partially full balloons. If the dart is thrown with an arc, it doesn't have to pierce the latex to pop the balloon. As it falls from above, the dart catches on the latex and causes it to tear.

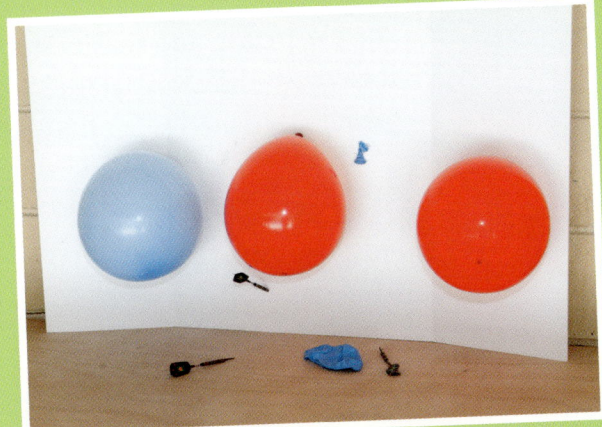

13

World-Saving Water Filter

In many countries, clean water isn't always available for people to drink. Engineers use science to turn water from dirty to drinkable. Recruit a friend to learn this simple way to help clean water.

Supplies

- about 2 handfuls of dirt, leaves, or pebbles you find outside
- 1 quart (1 liter) pitcher of water
- dry-ingredient measuring cups
- 1 cup (240 mL) activated carbon (also called activated charcoal)
- gallon size plastic zip-top bag
- scissors
- empty 2-liter soda bottle
- ruler
- white cotton T-shirt, no decorations
- 2 cups (480 mL) clean gravel
- 2 cups (480 mL) clean sand
- drinking glass

1. Dump the dirt, leaves, and pebbles into the pitcher of water. Set it aside.

2. Pour the activated charcoal into the plastic bag and seal it. Step on it to crush the charcoal into small, gravel-sized pieces. Set it aside.

3. Carefully cut off the bottom of the soda bottle.

14

4 Cut an 8-inch (20-cm) square from the T-shirt. Have someone hold the edges of the square like a basket. Carefully pour the clean gravel into the square. Then gently place the square with gravel into the bottle over the pouring hole.

5 Add the crushed charcoal on top of the gravel. Then pour the clean sand on top.

6 Place the drinking glass under the pouring hole on the bottle. Slowly pour the pitcher of dirty water through the filter. Watch to see if the water comes out clean or cloudy.

Insider Info

Science explains how the dirty water went from dangerous to drinkable. The rocks, dirt, and leaves were trapped by the gravel and sand. But the dirt also had **contaminants** in it that we couldn't see. Bacteria and other microscopic creatures live in dirt. If swallowed, they could make a person sick. The layer of activated charcoal attracted those smaller contaminants. They chemically **bonded** to the carbon. The contaminants stayed in the filter instead of flowing out with the water.

Your filtered water is probably safe to drink. But without testing it for contaminants, you can't know for sure. It could take several rounds of filtering to make the water totally safe.

contaminant: something that makes something else unhealthy or unfit to use
bond: to stick together

15

Finding a Quiet Spot

Music pounds through the wall from your brother's stereo. You tell him it's too loud, but he insists you're being dramatic. Only solid proof will change his attitude. Gather your data with this device.

Supplies

- scissors
- large shoebox without lid
- golf pencil about 3½ inches (9 cm) long
- ruler
- small paper cup
- small piece of modeling clay
- 12-inch (30-cm) piece of string
- piece of white paper
- 5–10 marbles

1. Use the scissors to cut away both long sides of the box. Leave the short sides and bottom attached. Then use a pencil to poke two holes about 1 inch (2.5 cm) apart in the center of the box's bottom. Place the box upside down on a table, so the bottom becomes the top.

2. With a pencil, poke one hole in the center of the paper cup. Poke one hole right under the rim of the cup and another opposite it.

3. From inside the cup, push the pencil through the bottom hole. Push it just far enough that the point sticks out the bottom. Inside the cup, put clay around the pencil to keep it in place.

4. Measure and cut the string. Pull it through the two holes near the cup's rim.

5 Set the cup under the box. Thread the left side of the string through the left hole in the box. Do the same on the right side.

6 Pull up on the strings so the cup hangs evenly, and the pencil point is about ½ inch (1 cm) off the tabletop. Tie the string on top of the box to keep the cup in place. Help from a friend or family member will make this step easier.

7 Put a piece of paper under the pencil. Weigh down the cup with marbles so the pencil tip lightly touches the paper.

8 Leave the box in a spot that tends to be noisy. When you return, see if the pencil has drawn lines on the paper. The more lines you find, the noisier that spot is.

Insider Info

The device you made is a simple seismometer. This machine measures sound waves moving through the air. Noises are made by **vibrations**. Your vocal cords vibrate when you speak. Stereo speakers vibrate when electric signals are pushed into them. The vibrations move through the air in waves. When the waves reach a solid object they cause the object to vibrate. When sound waves reached the marble-filled cup, they caused it to vibrate and move on the string. The vibrating cup made the pencil move around the paper. The louder something is, the stronger its sound waves are. Loud sounds will cause more vibrations and more pencil marks.

Engineers use seismometers in the real world to measure sound waves caused by earthquakes. They use that information to create buildings that won't collapse during a quake.

vibration: a fast movement back and forth

New Jewelry from Old CDs

Your musical tastes might change, but your need for cool accessories never will. Don't toss unwanted music CDs. Turn them into wearable art.

Supplies

- scissors
- music CD
- ruler
- nail file
- drill with a small bit ($1/16$-inch or smaller)
- 2 feet (.6 m) of thin jewelry cord
- paint, glitter, and other decorations

1. Use scissors to cut a wedge out of the CD. Make the wedge about 1 inch (2.5 cm) wide at the center of the CD. The curved outer edge should be 2 inches (5 cm) wide.

2. Use a nail file to smooth the top, sides, and corners of the wedge piece.

3. Have an adult drill two small holes on the short side of the wedge piece. One should be near the top left corner. The other should be directly across it near the top right corner.

18

4. Thread the cord through the left hole from front to back. Thread it back through the right hole and pull it until both sides are even in length. Tie the ends in a knot.

5. Decorate the wedge to fit your style. Let it dry completely before you wear your new necklace.

Insider Info

Using the right materials is an important part of engineering new products. Materials have properties that help or hinder the final product. For example, in this project there's a reason it was important to use a music CD. If you used a CD-R, or recordable disc, the project wouldn't have worked. The layers of CD-R discs peel apart when cut. But music CDs can be cut without risk of peeling. The two types of discs are actually made differently. Music CDs are pressed in a process called injection molding. This process keeps the layers on a CD together.

Engineers must choose the right materials when they are making new products. They don't want things peeling apart if they're supposed to stay together!

Tie-Dyed Engineering

Longing for a new look? Here's a simple way to create your own fashion line. Your retro style will be all the rage.

Supplies
- plastic cup
- white cotton T-shirt
- rubber band
- permanent markers in your favorite colors
- cotton swaps
- rubbing alcohol

1. Turn the plastic cup upside down. Put it inside the T-shirt in a section you want to color. Hold the material in place by putting a rubber band around the shirt and cup.

2. Use one of the markers to make a circle of dots on the shirt. The circle should be about the size of a quarter in the cup's center.

3. Use a cotton swap to put four drops of rubbing alcohol in the center of the circle. Let the alcohol absorb into the material.

4. The ink from the markers will start to spread out. After the ink is finished spreading, add four more drops of alcohol in the center of the circle to make the pattern larger. Let the shirt sit for about five minutes.

5. Repeat steps 1–4 wherever you want some color on the shirt.

6. Let the shirt dry overnight. Don't skimp on this dry time. The alcohol will be flammable if it's not dry. When it's dry, put the shirt in a dryer to set the colors. Use a high setting for about 15 minutes.

Insider Info

This shirt is a wearable example of a process called chromatography. In this process, you separated the **molecules** in the permanent ink. Ink molecules are a mixture of alcohol and colored **pigments**. In the project the ink's alcohol molecules were attracted to the rubbing alcohol molecules. The ink's alcohol dissolved into the rubbing alcohol. Then as the alcohol molecules spread out on the fabric, they pulled along the colored pigments.

Chemical engineers use this same process. They use chromatography to identify the molecules in dyes, foods, and medicines.

molecule: a group of two or more atoms bonded together
pigment: a substance that gives something a particular color

21

S'mores from the Sun

Who needs a campfire to make s'mores? Build your own solar cooker and have them anytime. Solar cookers work slowly, so plan to start around noon. Depending on the temperature outside, it may be several hours before your treat is ready to eat. But the project is so cool, it will be worth the wait.

Supplies

- marker
- cardboard pizza box cleaned of crumbs and cheese
- ruler
- scissors
- aluminum foil
- masking tape
- plastic wrap
- black construction paper
- butter knife
- measuring spoons
- 4 teaspoons (20 mL) raspberry preserves
- 8 graham cracker squares
- 4 chocolate kisses
- 4 marshmallows
- stick

1. Draw a square on the lid of the pizza box about 1 inch (2.5 cm) from the edge on all sides. Create a flap by cutting the square on three sides. Do not cut the side where the box hinges.

2. Close the box, and lift the flap. Cover the bottom side of the flap with foil, folding the foil over the edges. Smooth out wrinkles and secure with tape.

3. Open the box. Cover the hole created by the flap with plastic wrap. Stretch it tight and secure with tape. Make sure no air can get through the edges. Repeat with a second piece of plastic wrap over the first piece.

4. Cover the inside of the box with foil. Fold foil over the sides and smooth wrinkles. Secure with tape on the outside.

continue on next page

5 Cover the foil in the bottom of the box with black construction paper. The paper should mostly cover the foil, but does not have to fit exactly. Secure with tape.

6 Cut a 10-inch (25-cm) square piece of foil. Put it in the center of the pizza box.

7 Spread 1 teaspoon (5 mL) of preserves on each of four graham cracker squares. Put chocolate kisses on top of the preserves. Top each s'more with a marshmallow and another cracker. Place the s'mores on the foil square in the box.

8 Close the box, and head outside to find a sunny spot.

9 Open the flap and position it to reflect sunlight onto the plastic wrap. Prop the flap in place with a stick and adjust positioning as needed.

10 Leave the box in place. Check the s'mores at least every hour. As the temperature in the oven rises, the chocolate and marshmallows will begin to melt. Don't open the lid with the plastic wrap so heat doesn't escape. Watch for melting through the plastic wrap window. When your s'mores are nice and melty, then open the box and get your treats.

Insider Info

With your homemade solar cooker, you harness heat from the sun. The foil on the flap reflects sunlight into the box. The black paper inside absorbs the sunlight. As the sunlight is absorbed, it becomes **thermal energy**. The thermal energy raises the temperature of the paper. The paper then radiates heat into the cooker. The plastic wrap creates a seal so the heat is trapped inside the box. This seal causes the temperature inside to rise. The high temperature is enough to melt marshmallows.

This solar cooker is just one small way to use the sun's energy. Engineers work on projects to find ways to use solar energy to power our world.

thermal energy: the flow of energy from one thing to another that causes a change in temperature

Alarming Fun

You can't always be home to prevent siblings from snooping in your stuff. But you can create an alarm to remind them it's off limits.

Supplies

- wire stripper or knife
- small electric 1.5 volt buzzer with wires attached
- 12 inches (30 cm) of electrical wire
- electrical tape
- AA battery
- 10-inch (25-cm) square wood board
- scissors
- 4-inch (10-cm) square of thin cardboard
- wooden clothespin that opens with a hinge
- 3 feet (.9 m) of string
- white glue

1. Have an adult strip away 1 inch (2.5 cm) of insulation from the ends of the buzzer wires. Also strip away 1 inch (2.5 cm) of insulation from each end of the electrical wire.

2. Using electrical tape, secure the battery to the upper left-hand corner of the board. Tape the buzzer to the board's upper right-hand corner. If the buzzer wires are too short to reach the battery, move the buzzer closer to the battery.

3. Use electrical tape to secure one buzzer wire to the positive end of the battery. Secure one end of the electrical wire to the battery's negative end. Make sure the metal of the wires touches the battery.

4. Use scissors to poke a small hole in the center of the cardboard.

5. Pinch the clothespin so it opens. Wrap the free end of the electrical wire around one side of the open pin. The exposed wire should be on the inside of the pin.

6. Wrap the free wire from the buzzer around the other side of the open clothespin. Make sure the exposed wires touch when the pin is closed. This should cause the buzzer to sound.

continue on next page

7 Close the clothespin on the cardboard. The cardboard should go between the wires to prevent them from touching. The cardboard should stop the alarm from buzzing.

8 Knot one end of the string several times so the knot is too big to go through the cardboard's hole. Thread the string through the hole from back to front.

9 Glue the clothespin to the center of the wood board. Place it on its side, so it can open and close.

10 Close your door, and tie the other end of the string to the doorknob. Lay the board on the floor near the door inside your room. Make sure the string is tight. If the door is pulled from the outside, the string will pull the cardboard out of the clothespin. When the pin closes, the wires will touch. The buzzer will sound until you open the clothespin again.

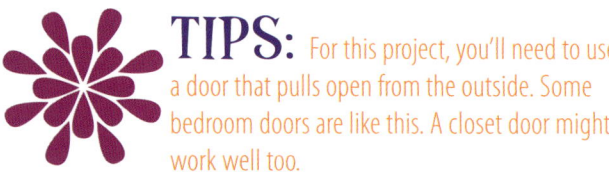

TIPS: For this project, you'll need to use a door that pulls open from the outside. Some bedroom doors are like this. A closet door might work well too.

Keeping the alarm in position when you leave the room might be tricky. Go slowly, and open the door as little as possible.

Insider Info

Alarms are just one way engineers put electricity to practical use. Your alarm works because it is designed as a closed **circuit**. It works the same way household lamps and car headlights do. On a closed circuit, electrical **current** flows continuously, starting and ending at the same point. In this alarm the battery creates the electrical current. When the wires in the clothespin touch, the current flows from the battery through the wires. When the current reaches the buzzer, it begins to sound. Then the current returns to the battery and continues the cycle over and over. The buzzer continues to sound until something interrupts the flow of electricity. When you open the clothespin, the wires no longer touch, and the buzzer stops buzzing.

circuit: a path for electricity to flow through
current: the flow of electricity

Glossary

accelerate (ak-SEL-uh-rate)—to speed up

bond (BAHND)—to stick together

circuit (SUHR-kuht)—a path for electricity to flow through

contaminant (kuhn-TAM-uh-nuhnt)—something that makes something else unhealthy or unfit to use

current (KUHR-uhnt)—the flow of electricity

friction (FRIK-shuhn)—a force created when two objects rub together; friction slows down objects

innovation (in-uh-VAY-shuhn)—a new idea or invention

molecule (MOL-uh-kyool)—the atoms making up the smallest unit of a substance; H20 is a molecule of water

pigment (PIG-muhnt)—a substance that gives something a particular color

stabilize (STEY-buh-lahyz)—to make firm and steady

thermal energy (THUR-muhl EN-ur-jee)—the flow of energy from one thing to another that causes a change in temperature

vibration (vye-BRAY-shuhn)—a fast movement back and forth

Read More

Ebner, Aviva, ed. *Engineering Science Experiments.* Experiments for Future Scientists. New York: Chelsea House, 2011.

Enz, Tammy. *Zoom It: Invent New Machines that Move.* Invent It. Mankato, Minn.: Capstone Press, 2012.

Herweck, Don. *Mechanical Engineering.* Mission Science. Mankato, Minn.: Compass Point Books, 2009.

Internet Sites

FactHound offers a safe, fun way to find Internet sites related to this book. All of the sites on FactHound have been researched by our staff.

Here's all you do:

Visit www.facthound.com

Type in this code: 9781429676779

Check out projects, games and lots more at
www.capstonekids.com

Index

balloons, 12–13

chemical bonds, 15
chromatography, 21
circuits, 29
contact area, 7
contaminants, 15

electric current, 29
ethylene, 9

friction, 7

injection molding, 19

load distribution, 11

materials, 19
molecules, 21

packaging, 9
pigments, 21

respiration, 9

seismometers, 17
solar energy, 25
sound waves, 17
stress, 13

thermal energy, 25

vibrations, 17
vocal cords, 17